Rookie
Get Ready to Code™

Be Smart
Online

by Marcie Flinchum Atkins

Content Consultant

Sarah Otts
Scratch Online Community Developer
MIT Media Lab, Massachusetts Institute of Technology

Reading Consultant

Jeanne M. Clidas, Ph.D.
Reading Specialist

Children's Press®
An Imprint of Scholastic Inc.

Library of Congress Cataloging-in-Publication Data
Names: Atkins, Marcie Flinchum, author.
Title: Be smart online/by Marcie Flinchum Atkins.
Description: New York, NY: Children's Press, an imprint of Scholastic Inc.,
[2019] | Series: Rookie get ready to code | Includes index.
Identifiers: LCCN 2018030276| ISBN 9780531132289 (library binding) | ISBN 9780531137031 (pbk.)
Subjects: LCSH: Internet and children—Juvenile literature. | Internet—Safety measures—Juvenile literature. |
Online social networks—Safety measures—Juvenile literature.
Classification: LCC HQ784.I58 A83 2019 | DDC 004.67/8083—dc23

Produced by Spooky Cheetah Press
Creative Direction: Judith E. Christ for Scholastic Inc.
Design: Anna Tunick Tabachnik

Published in 2019 by Children's Press, an imprint of Scholastic Inc.

Printed in North Mankato, MN, USA 113

SCHOLASTIC, CHILDREN'S PRESS, GET READY TO CODE™, and associated logos are trademarks and/or
registered trademarks of Scholastic Inc.

1 2 3 4 5 6 7 8 9 10 R 28 27 26 25 24 23 22 21 20 19

Scholastic Inc., 557 Broadway, New York, NY 10012.

Photos ©: cover: andresr/iStockphoto; cover background: RioAbajoRio/Shutterstock; cover and throughout
robots: the8monkey/iStockphoto; inside cover and throughout: pmmix/Shutterstock; 4: Andegraund548/
Dreamstime; 5: monkeybusinessimages/iStockphoto; 6: Rachel Macreadie/EyeEm/Getty Images; 9 email:
Devonyu/iStockphoto; 9 instagram: Hadrian/Shutterstock; 9 text: Prykhodov/iStockphoto; 9 snapchat:
dennizn/Shutterstock; 9 youtube: PixieMe/Shutterstock; 10: leolintang/Shutterstock; 13 phone: Leonardo255/
Dreamstime; 13 legos: Just dance/Shutterstock; 15: Westend61/Getty Images; 15 inset screen: filistimlyanin/
iStockphoto; 19 boy: Morsa Images/Getty Images; 19 arrow cursor: MicroOne/Shutterstock; 20: Rafa
artphoto/Shutterstock; 20 inset screen: rawf8/Shutterstock; 23: Jamie Grill/Getty Images; 25: Hero
Images/Getty Images; 26-27: LWA/Dann Tardif/Getty Images; 28: Bigshots/Getty Images;
29: Bigshots/Getty Images.

TABLE OF CONTENTS

Chapter 1

Your Digital Footprint

There are many things you can do on the Internet—play games, do homework, watch videos, and communicate with family and friends. Those are all lots of fun. But you have to be careful. You need to learn how to use the Internet safely.

When you walk on the beach or step in mud, you leave a footprint. When you go online, you also leave a footprint. It is a **digital** footprint. A footprint in the sand or mud disappears after a while. A digital footprint never goes away.

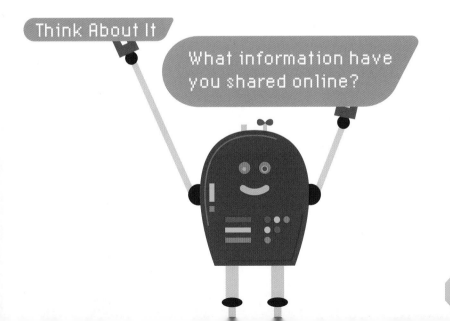

Think About It

What information have you shared online?

Sending a text, visiting a website, and searching the web all leave digital footprints. The same goes for sending an email or photo or participating in a video game chat. Some of the things people post online can be seen by anyone—even strangers.

What applications (apps) do you use that leave a digital footprint?

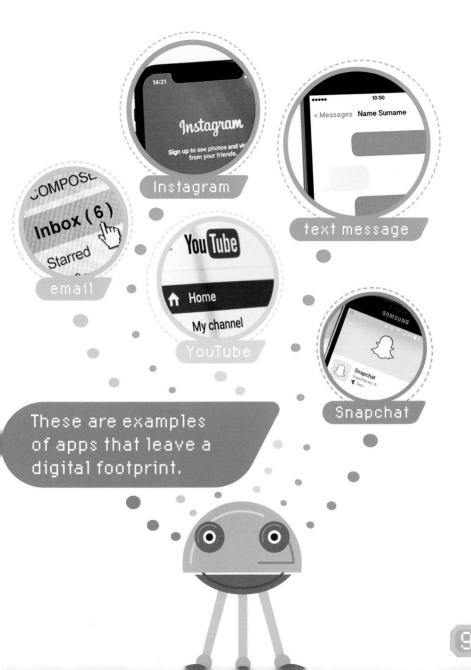

Instagram

text message

email

YouTube

Snapchat

These are examples of apps that leave a digital footprint.

9

You must be at least 13 years old to sign up for many online accounts. Even then, an adult should always know what accounts you have open. A parent or caregiver should also know what you are posting.

You should also think carefully about what you post.

Questions to Ask *Before* Posting

Does it give away private information?

Will the post embarrass someone, or could it hurt their feelings?

Did I ask for permission?

If you can answer no, no, and yes, it is safe to post!

Chapter 2

Passwords and Privacy

Private information is information that is unique to you. It can help identify you and where you are located. It can allow others to find out too much about you. You should never post private information online.

Keep your private information private!

Examples of private information:

- phone number
- full name
- birth date
- address
- password
- school
- names of your family members
- names of your pets

Which post is safe to share online?

"Playing with Legos!"

"Sam Shelham is playing with Legos!"

We use **passwords** to get into our computers and online accounts. But they are really meant to keep *others* out! A password keeps your private information private. It is important to have a password that no one else can guess. You should share your password only with your parents or caregivers.

Ask your parent or caregiver to keep all your passwords together in a safe place.

Username

user

Password

●●●●●●●●●●●●●●

Many people use "123456" and "password" as their passwords. These are not good. They are too easy to guess. How do you create a strong password? Here are some tips:

- Do not use private information in your password (for example, name, birth date).
- Use at least eight letters or numbers.
- Use a different password for every site.
- Include special symbols ($ % *), capital letters, and numbers.

And remember, share your passwords only with a parent or caregiver.

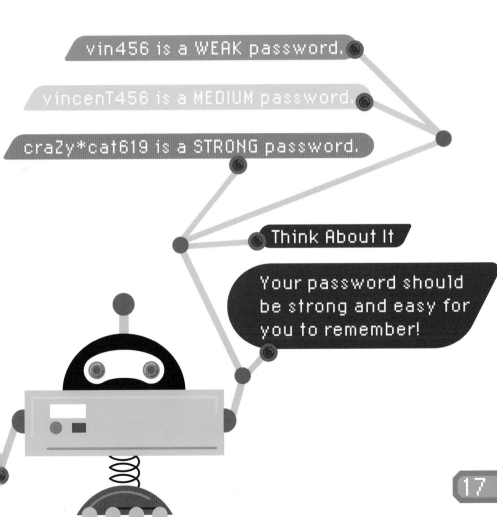

vin456 is a WEAK password.

vincenT456 is a MEDIUM password.

craZy*cat619 is a STRONG password.

Think About It

Your password should be strong and easy for you to remember!

Chapter 3

Be Smart About Downloads

There are lots of fun things on the Internet. Quizzes, games, and apps are just a few examples. But you need to be careful when you use them. Do not take quizzes that ask for your private information. Ask a grown-up before you **download** a new game or app. Your parents or caregivers need

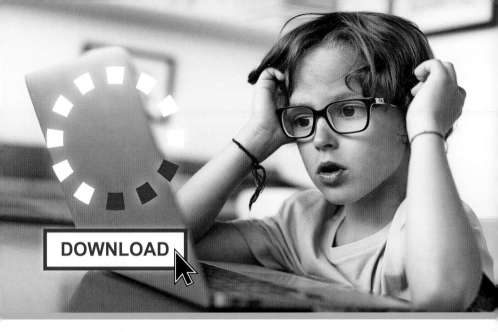

DOWNLOAD

to make sure it is right for you. They also need to make sure it is safe to download.

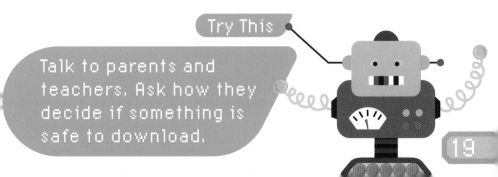

Try This

Talk to parents and teachers. Ask how they decide if something is safe to download.

Don't worry: *You cannot get sick from a computer virus!*

Viruses are programs that can steal information from your computer. They can also cause it to crash or shut down. You can get viruses from downloading files or clicking links from someone you don't know.

Hackers try to steal people's private information. They might use your name to open online accounts and pretend to be you. Never download files from someone you do not know. Do not download any files that you were not expecting.

Chapter 4

Digital Citizenship

When we are good citizens, we are kind and helpful to others. We make responsible decisions. When we are good digital citizens, we use those same skills online. We are kind to people we talk to online. We never tease or say mean words to others online. And we never share a

picture of someone online without his
or her permission.

Even if you are careful, you can get into a sticky situation online. You may feel unsafe or uncomfortable. You might not know what to do. If that happens, tell a trusted adult. If a classmate sends something inappropriate or mean to you, tell an adult. If a stranger tries to contact you, tell an adult. Don't be afraid to let teachers or your parents handle the situation.

Think About It

What adults can you talk to about an online situation?

The Internet is a great tool. You can use it to learn many new things and to play games. As you get older, you will use it to communicate with friends. If you make smart decisions, you will stay safe online.

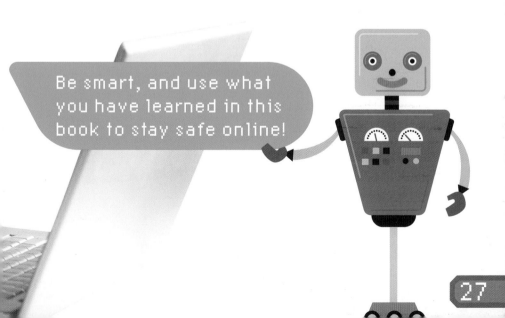

Be smart, and use what you have learned in this book to stay safe online!

SPOT THE PROBLEM

Look at this photo and caption that were posted online. What details should have been left out?

And the birthday boy wins: Diego Sanchez does it again!

ORANGE ELEMENTARY

2

1/12/19

Diego is giving his first and last names.

The photo shows the date, so Diego has told people his birth date by calling himself the "birthday boy."

Diego's school name shows where he lives.

And the birthday boy wins! Diego Sanchez does it again!

2
ORANGE ELEMENTARY

school name

full name

date stamp 1/12/19

DIGITAL DECISIONS QUIZ

Can you answer these questions about online safety correctly?

1 **Ali just changed his password at school to "password." What should he do?**

    a) Change his password to his name and birth date.
    b) Ask his friend to give him a new password idea.
    c) Change his password to be harder to guess.

2 **Angelina got a text message from someone she doesn't know. What should she do?**

    a) Tell a parent.   b) Ignore it.   c) Text them back.

3 **A stranger is trying to chat with Ethan on a video game. What should he do?**

    a) Chat with the stranger.
    b) Tell a parent.
    c) Invite a friend to join the chat.

GLOSSARY

digital (**dij**-uh-tuhl)
related to computers, including the Internet

download (**down**-lode)
save something from the Internet onto your computer

hackers (**hak**-urz)
experts at getting into computer systems illegally

passwords (**pass**-wurdz)
secret words, codes, or phrases that you need to know to
get into a computer system

viruses (**vye**-rhuss-ez)
hidden instructions within a computer program designed to
destroy a computer or damage information on a computer

How Did You Do?

The answers are c; a; b.
How many did you get right?

INDEX

FACTS FOR NOW

Visit this Scholastic website for more information
on being smart online: **www.factsfornow.scholastic.com**
Enter the keywords **Smart Online**

ABOUT THE AUTHOR

Marcie Flinchum Atkins teaches kids how to use computers and find the best books in her job as an elementary librarian. She holds an M.A. and an M.F.A. in children's literature, and lives with her family in Virginia. Read more about Marcie at www.marcieatkins.com.